Basic Steps for Making a Punch Project

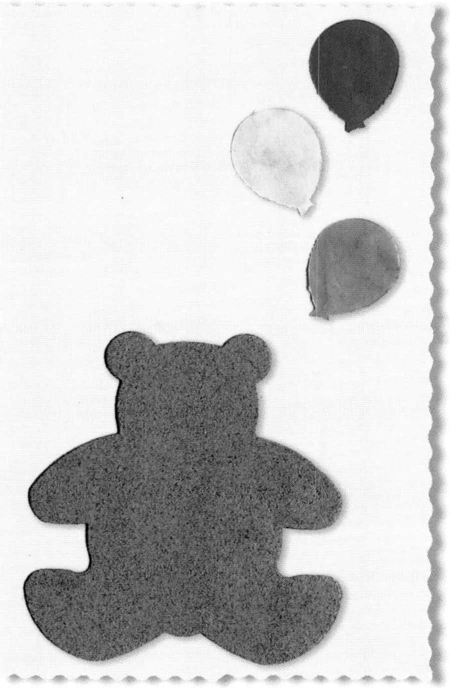

Balloon Bear - 1⅝" bear, ⅛" circle, ¼" oval, ⁵⁄₁₆" oval, ⅝" balloon punches - Brown, Black and White gel pens, Pink and Brown chalk

1. Plain punch art bear with vellum balloons

2. Punch art bear shaded with chalk creates dimension.

Nursery Bear - 1⅝" bear, ⅛" circle, ³⁄₁₆" circle, ⅞" bow, ⁵⁄₁₆" oval punches - Gray gel pen, Blue and Pink chalk

Nursery Bunny - 1⅝" bear, ⅛" circle, ³⁄₁₆" circle, ⅞" bow, ⅝" heart, ⁵⁄₁₆" oval, ½" oval punches - Gray and Pink gel pens, Pink chalk

Party Hat - 2" circle, ⅝" sun, ⁵⁄₁₆" spiral punches - Black gel pen, Black chalk

Party Cupcake - 2" circle, cloud cartoon bubble, ⅝" teardrop, ⁵⁄₁₆" spiral, ⅞" rectangle, fleur de lis border punches - Black gel pen, Black chalk

Bear Cub - 1⅝" bear, ⅝" circle, ¼" sun, ½" oval, ¼" oval punches - Black and Brown gel pens, Brown chalk

Puppy - 1⅝" bear, ⅝" circle, 1" circle, ⅝" pawprint, ½" oval, ¼" sun punches - Black, Brown and White gel pens, Pink and Brown chalk

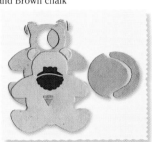

Lion Cub - 1⅝" bear, ⅛" circle, ½" circle, 1" circle, ¼" sun, 1¼" sun, ⅝" pawprint, ⁵⁄₁₆" flower punches - Black, Pink and Gray gel pens, Black chalk. Hint: Glue my ears on top of my mane and make me roar!

Kitten - 1⅝" bear, ⅝" circle, 1" circle, ⅝" shell, ³⁄₁₆" triangle punches - Black, Gray and Pink gel pens, Gray chalk

Baby Mouse - 1⅝" bear, ⅝" circle, 1" oval, swirl border #4, ¼" oval, ⅝" cloud punches - Black, Pink and Gray gel pens, Black chalk

Boy Bunny - 1⅝" bear, ⅛" circle, ³⁄₁₆" circle, 1" frame fleur de lis, ½" heart, ⅝" strawberry, ⅝" footprint punches - Black, Pink, Yellow and Gray gel pens, Blue and Gray chalk

Piglet - 1⅝" bear, ¼" circle, ⁵⁄₁₆" circle, ⅝" circle, ⅜" heart, ³⁄₁₆" triangle, ⁵⁄₁₆" spiral, ⅝" shell punches - Black gel pen, Pink and Gray chalk

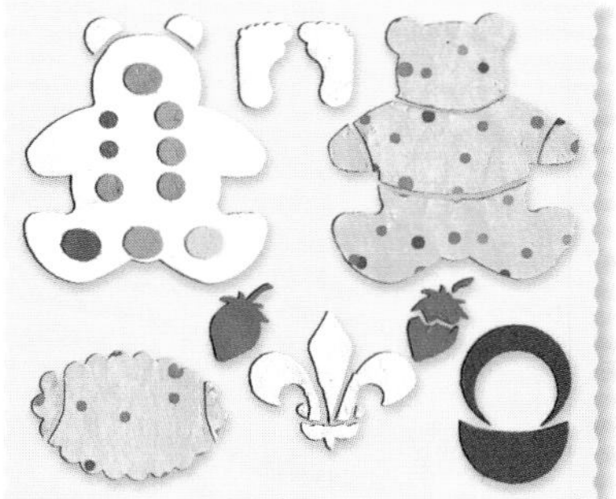

Girl Bunny - 1⅝" bear, ⅛" circle, ³⁄₁₆" circle, ¾" circle, 1" frame fleur de lis, ⅝" strawberry, 1¼" scallop oval, ⁵⁄₁₆" oval, ⅝" footprint punches - Black, Pink, Purple and Gray gel pens, Purple and Gray chalk

Moo Calf - 1⅝" bear, ⁵⁄₁₆" circle, ⅝" circle, ¼" moon, ⅜" heart, ⅜" apple, swirl border #1, ⅜" snowflake punches - Black, Brown and White gel pens, Pink and Brown chalk

Devil Baby - 1⅝" bear, ⅝" circle, ³⁄₁₆" triangle, ¼" moon, ⅛" heart, swirl border #1 punches - Black gel pen, Black ch

Animals & Such

Love Bear - 1⅝" bear, 1⁷⁄₁₆" heart, 2" heart, ⁵⁄₁₆" oval, ¼" oval, ¼" sun, ¼" lips, butterflies border punches, ½" letter stickers - Purple, Black and Brown gel pens, Pink, Black and Brown chalk

Barefoot Boy - 1⅝" bear, ⅛" circle, ½" circle, ⅝" sun, ⅝" fish, 1" oval, ⅝" footprint, Vivaldi border, fishing pole border punches - Black, Orange and Silver gel pens, Black and Pink chalk

Girl Ice Skater - 1⅝" bear, 1⁷⁄₁₆" heart, grandma's lace border, ⅞" sleigh, ⅜" birch leaf, ¼" flower punches - Tiny scallop wavy scissors, White, Black and Yellow gel pens, Pink, Black and Brown chalk

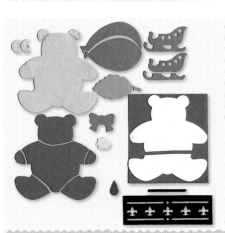

Holiday Elf - 1⅝" bear, 1¼" balloon, ⅝" birch leaf, ⅞" sleigh, ½" bow, ⁵⁄₁₆" teardrop, ⁵⁄₁₆" mini house, fleur de lis border punches - Red, Black, Yellow and Green gel pens, Pink, Black and Brown chalk

Helpful Hints

Placement. Turn a paper punch upside down on your work table. Insert paper to accurately see what is being punched. Place paper in punch with the guidelines showing.

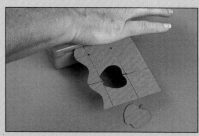

Punching. To punch a small shape inside a large shape, punch small the shape first then the large shape around it. Press down on the back of punch with the heel of your hand.

Adhesive. Zig 2-Way glue is photo-safe. The pen-tip applicator works well for small shapes. Dot adhesive on the shape and apply to paper immediately.

Tips. Use tweezers to hold small punched shapes when gluing.
Hint. Use photo tape or 'Sticky Dots' in place of glue.

Tips for Vellum: Use punched vellum for designs with a transparent effect like water or glass.

Baby Talk

Pieces from border and corner punches make great decorations. They can even help tie your shoes!

Oval cartoon bubble punch

5Bib - 1" circle, 2" circle, 5/16" square punches - Pink and Blue gel pens, Pink chalk

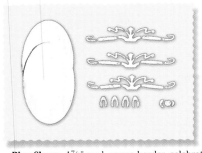 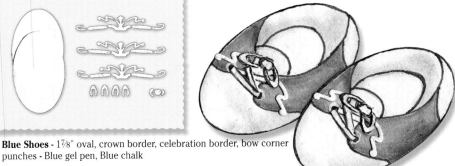

Blue Shoes - 1 7/8" oval, crown border, celebration border, bow corner punches - Blue gel pen, Blue chalk

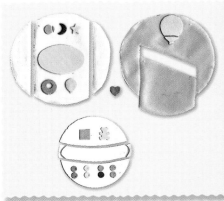

Baby Bottle - 1/8" circle, 3/16" circle, 5/16" circle, 1 1/2" circle, 2" circle, 1" oval, 1/4" moon, 3/16" star, 5/8" balloon, 1/4" balloon, 1/4" bear, 1/4" square, 1/4" heart punches - Black, White, Pink, Blue and Gray gel pens, Orange and Blue chalk, Clear and Blue vellum

Fancy Slippers - 1 7/8" oval, 1/2" bow punches - Pink and Black gel pens, Gray chalk

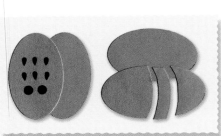 

Pink Slippers - 1 7/8" oval, heart and tears border, 3/16" circle punches - Pink and Purple gel pens, Purple chalk

Rattle - 1/2" circle, 3/4" circle, 1 1/4" circle, 7/8" bow, 1/4" heart punches - White gel pen, Purple chalk, 1/4" x 1 1/2" strip of paper
Hint: Apply hearts randomly, trim edges that overlap.

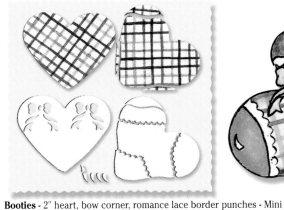 

Booties - 2" heart, bow corner, romance lace border punches - Mini scallop scissors, Black, Blue, Yellow and Pink gel pens, Blue, Pink and Yellow chalk

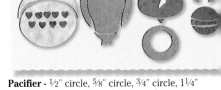

Pacifier - 1/2" circle, 5/8" circle, 3/4" circle, 1 1/4" circle, 1" oval ornament, 1/2" bow, 1 1/4" balloon, 1/8" heart, lace edge teardrop corner punches - Pink and Blue chalk

Baby Title - ⅞" heart, ½" bow, 1/16" circle punches - Pink gel pen, Pink, Blue and Yellow chalk, Hand cut ribbon, ½" letter stickers

I'm so easy! Just punch an opening for my face with a small circle punch.

Baby Bunting - 1⅝" bear, ⅛" heart, ½" circle, ⅝" circle, oval cartoon bubble punches - Silver and Pink gel pens, Pink chalk

Baby Boy - 1⅝" bear, ⅛" circle, 3/16" circle, 1" bell punches - Black gel pen, Pink and Blue chalk

Baby Girl - 1⅝" bear, 1¼" balloon, ⅛" circle, ½" bow, ¼" sun punches - Black gel pen, Pink and Purple chalk

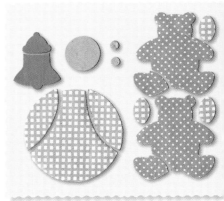

Use a 'bubble' to make such a simple title!

Oval cartoon bubble punch

Sweet Dreams - $1/8$" circle, $5/8$" circle, $1 1/4$" circle, $1 1/4$" scallop oval punches - Black gel pen, Pink and Blue chalk, $1/2$" letter stickers, Blue vellum

Special Delivery - $3/16$" circle, $3/4$" circle, 2" circle, $1 5/8$" bear, $1/2$" oval, 1" bell punches - Black gel pen, Pink, Blue and Green chalk

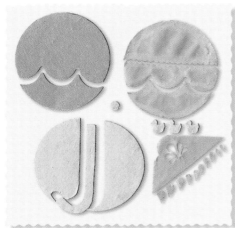

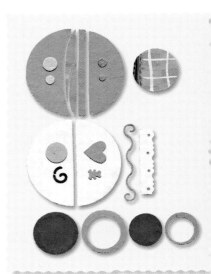

Parasol - $3/16$" circle, 2" circle, lace edge teardrop corner, $5/16$" duck punches - Black, Blue, and Orange gel pens, Gold, Pink and Purple chalk, Blue vellum

Baby Carriage - $1/8$" circle, $3/16$" circle, $5/16$" circle, $1/2$" circle, $3/4$" circle, 1" circle, 2" circle, $5/8$" heart, $1/4$" bear, swirl border #4 punches - $3/8$" x $1 1/2$" paper strip, Black gel pen, Pink and Blue chalk, Blue vellum, decorative scissors

Bath Time - $1/8$" circle, $3/16$" circle, $5/16$" circle, $5/8$" circle, 2" circle, $1/4$" heart, $5/16$" spiral, $1/2$" rectangle, $1/2$" duck, baroque border punches - Black, Blue and Orange gel pens, Blue, Pink and Gray chalk, Pink and Blue vellum

Bubble Baby - $1 1/2$" angel, $1/2$" duck, $3/16$" circle, $1/4$" circle, $1 7/8$" cloud, lace edge teardrop corner punches - Black, Orange and Blue gel pens, Pink, Blue and Yellow chalk, Pink and Blue vellum

Baby Shower - $3/4$" square, 1" bear, $1/2$" heart, $9/16$" umbrella, $1/2$" sun punches - Black, Blue and Pink gel pens, Pink, Gold and Purple chalk

Time for a Change - $1\frac{1}{2}$" angel, $1/8$" circle, $5/8$" circle, 2" circle, $9/16$" square, $1\frac{9}{16}$" square, $9/16$" elephant, $1/8$" heart, $5/8$" shell, romance lace border punches - Black, Pink, Gray, Blue and Purple gel pens, Pink, Yellow, Purple, Green, Blue and Brown chalk

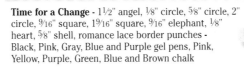

Gift Border - $3/4$" square, $1/2$" bow, $1/4$" bear punches - Hand cut wave, Pink, Blue, Yellow, Purple and Green chalk

Smiley Grads - 1⅛" smiley face, 2" heart, 3/16" circle, ¾" circle, 1" circle, 1¼" scallop oval, ⅝" cloud, ⅞" bell, ⅝" egg, ⅝" shell, ¼" footprint, ⅞" rectangle punches - Black, White, Blue and Red gel pens, Gray, Pink and Peach chalk

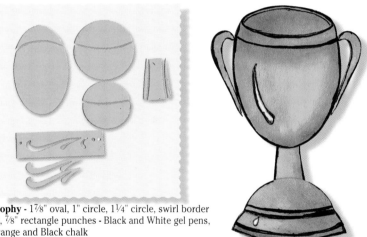

Trophy - 1⅞" oval, 1" circle, 1¼" circle, swirl border #2, ⅞" rectangle punches - Black and White gel pens, Orange and Black chalk

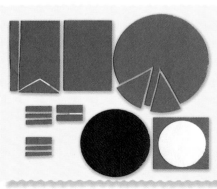

Blue Ribbon - 1" circle, 1½" circle, 2" circle, ½" rectangle, 1½" rectangle punches - Black gel pen, Blue, Black and Gray chalk

Kids & Teens

Kids with Glasses - 5⁄16" circle, 1⁄2" circle, 5⁄8" circle, 2" circle, 1 1⁄8" smiley face, 1⁄4" sun, 5⁄16" oval, bunting border, fleur de lis border, romance lace border punches - Black and Brown gel pens, Pink and Brown chalk, Clear vellum

Soap -
Rectangle cartoon bubble, 1 1⁄4" scalloped oval, 1" oval, 5⁄16" circle, 3⁄8" circle, 1⁄2" circle punches - Black gel pen, Black chalk, Blue vellum Hint: To shadow an item, glue 2 identical shapes together and slide the top one up and to the side.

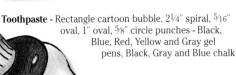

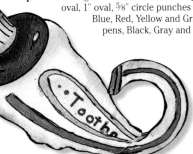

Sparkle Tooth - Rectangle cartoon bubble, 5⁄8" circle, 1 1⁄4" balloon, 5⁄8" star ornament, 1⁄4" square, 1⁄4" oval, romance lace border punches - Black, Gray and White gel pens, Pink and Gray chalk

Toothpaste - Rectangle cartoon bubble, 2 1⁄4" spiral, 5⁄16" oval, 1" oval, 5⁄8" circle punches - Black, Blue, Red, Yellow and Gray gel pens, Black, Gray and Blue chalk

After attaching the grass 'bristles', give this hair brush a trim!

Hair Brush - 1 7⁄8" oval, grass border punches - Black gel pen, Black chalk

oothbrush -
ectangle cartoon bubble, 7⁄8" rectan-
le, grass border punches - Black and
ellow gel pens, Black, chalk

Comb - Rectangle cartoon bubble, 1⁄4" rectangle punches - White gel pen

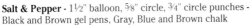

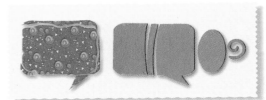

Salt & Pepper - 1½" balloon, ⅝" circle, ¾" circle punches - Black and Brown gel pens, Gray, Blue and Brown chalk

Tea Time - 1¼" balloon, 1⅛" bow, ⅝" spiral, ⅞" bell, ⁵⁄₁₆" oval punches - Black, Yellow, Purple and Teal gel pens, Purple chalk

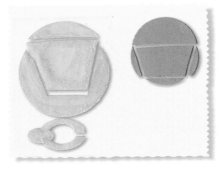

Measuring Cup - 2" circle, ½" oval, 1" oval punches - Black gel pen, Blue and Black chalk, Clear vellum

Sleeping Bag - Rectangle cartoon bubble, ⅝" spiral, 1" oval punches - Black gel pen, Black chalk

Teddy - 1" bear, 1" dress, ⅛" heart, ¼" oval punches - Black gel pen, Black and Purple chalk

Broken Egg - Cloud cartoon bubble, 1" oval punches - Black gel pen, Gray, Purple, Yellow and Orange chalk, Clear vellum

PJs - 1½" rectangle, 1" dress, bow corner punches - Black gel pen, Purple chalk

Whisk - ¾" hot air balloon repunched with ¾" regular balloon

Bowl & Whisk - 2" circle, cloud cartoon bubble, heart and tears border, ¾" hot air balloon, ³⁄₁₆" heart, ¾ balloon, 1" oval punches - Black gel pen, Blue, Black, Brown and Yellow chalk, Blue vellum

Slippers - 1⅛" footprint, ⅝" cloud punches - Black gel pen, Purple and Pink chalk

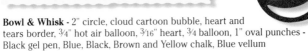

Oven Mitts - 1½" mittens, ⁵⁄₁₆" oval, ¼" oval punches - Black gel pen, Black chalk

Nightshirt - 2" circle, ⅜" square, ⅛" heart punches - Black and Purple gel pens, Purple chalk

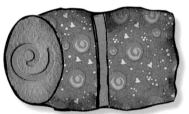

Party Pillow - Rectangle cartoon bubble, 5/8" teardrop punches - Pink and Purple gel pens, Blue chalk

TV - 1¼" square, 1⁹/₁₆" square, ⅛" circle, ³/₁₆" circle, ½" circle, fleur de lis border, butterflies border, corner rounder punches - Black gel pen, Purple and Blue chalk

Telephone - ⅛" circle, ⅝" circle, 1½" circle, ¼" rectangle, swirl border #4 punches - Black gel pen, Purple and Pink chalk

Cola - 2" circle, 1" oval, celebration border punches - Black gel pen, Black and Gray chalk

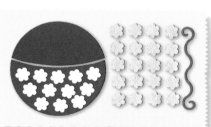

Popcorn - 2" circle, swirl border #4, ¼" flower punches - Black gel pen, Purple and Yellow chalk

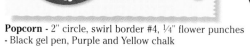

Christmas Candle - 1⅞" oval, fleur de lis border, ³⁄₁₆" circle, ⁵⁄₁₆" circle, ⅝" circle, 2" circle, ⅝" teardrop, ¼" heart, 1¼" holly, ¾" snow ornament punches - Black gel pen, Black, Brown and Orange chalk

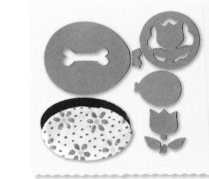

Gingerbread House - 1⁹⁄₁₆" square, ⅛" circle, ⁵⁄₁₆" circle, ½" circle, ⅜" snowflake, 1¾" snowflake, 1" oval, ⅞" rectangle, 1¼" scallop oval, ⅝" cloud, ⅝" flower, bow corner, swirl border #1 punches - Red, Green and White gel pens, Brown, Blue, Red and Black chalk

Reindeer in Mitten - 1½" mitten, ⅞" apple, ½" oval, ¼" oval, 1¼" dusty miller leaf, ⅜" birch leaf, ½" pine tree, ⅜" heart, ½" paw print punches - Black gel pen, Brown and Pink chalk

Turkey Dinner - 1"balloon, 2" balloon, 1" frame tulip, 1" bone, 1⅞" oval punches - Black and Blue gel pens, Brown and Blue chalk

Christmas Centerpiece - Rectangle cartoon bubble, corner rounder, fleur de lis border, ⅝" teardrop, 1¼" holly, ⅝" star ornament, ½" oval, ⅛" circle, ³⁄₁₆" circle, ¾" circle punches - Black gel pen, Green, Red and Black chalk
Hint: For poinsettias, glue ovals to back of star ornaments then glue on top of ¾" circle. Overlap ⅛" circles in center.

Holidays

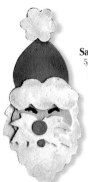

Santa - ½" heart, ⅝" balloon, ¼" flower, ½" maple leaf, ⅞" birch leaf, ¹⁄₁₆" circle, ⅛" circle punches - Black gel pen, Gray chalk

Hot Chocolate - 1¼" circle, 2" circle, ⅞" rectangle, ½" oval, 1" snowflake, ⁵⁄₁₆" spiral, 1¼" scallop oval punches - Brown and Red gel pens, Black, Gray and Blue chalk

Peppermint - 2" balloon, 1" circle punches - Black and Red gel pens, Blue chalk

Candy cane - 2" circle, ⅞" bow punches - Black, Green and Red gel pens, Black chalk

Oval cartoon bubble punch

Try this simple gingerbread 'recipe'.

Gingerbread Man - 1⅞" flower, ⅛" circle, ¾" circle, ³⁄₁₆" heart punches - Black, Red and White gel pens, Brown chalk

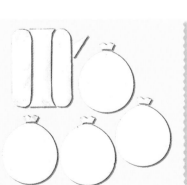

Wrapped Candies - Rectangle cartoon bubble, 1½" balloon punches - Black, Green and Red gel pens, Blue chalk

Heart Stocking - 2" heart, 1½" mitten, ⁵⁄₁₆" oval, ½" oval, ½" primitive heart, ⁵⁄₁₆" circle punches - Black gel pen, Black chalk

Small Santa - 1¼" scallop oval, 1¼" maple leaf, ⅞" fir tree, ⅞" heart, 1" balloon, ⁵⁄₁₆" flower, ⅛" circle, ³⁄₁₆" circle punches - Black gel pen, Gray chalk

Holidays

Mittens - 1½" mitten, ½" snowflake punches - Black gel pen, Black chalk

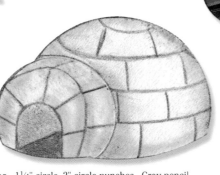

Igloo - 1¼" circle, 2" circle punches - Gray pencil, Pink, Blue and Gray chalk

Christmas Bells - 1" bell, 1¼" holly, ½" oval, 1" oval, ³⁄₁₆" circle, swirl border #1, swirl border #2 punches - Red and Black gel pens, Black chalk

Tree Santa - ⁵⁄₈" sun, 2" sun, 2" heart, ⅛" circle, ³⁄₁₆" circle, ¼" Christmas tree, 1¼" balloon, piney ridge corner, 1¼" scallop oval punches - Black gel pen, Gray, Brown and Pink chalk

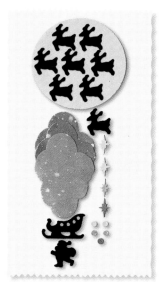

Moonlight Santa - 2" circle, 1⅞" cloud, ⅞" sleigh, ½" Santa, ½" reindeer, ⅝" star ornament, ⅛" circle punches - Black, Purple and Blue gel pens, Blue chalk

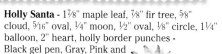

Holly Santa - 1⅞" maple leaf, ⅞" fir tree, ⅝" cloud, 5/16" oval, ¼" moon, ½" oval, ⅛" circle, 1¼" balloon, 2" heart, holly border punches - Black gel pen, Gray, Pink and Black chalk

Stocking Cap - 1" circle, 1¼" flower, ⅝" sun, ¼" sun punches - White, Red, Blue and Green gel pens, Blue and Black chalk

Rudolph - Rectangle cartoon bubble, ½" heart, 5/16" oval, 1" oval, 3/16" birch leaf, 1¼" dusty miller leaf, ⅞" apple, 1⅜" apple, ¼" Christmas tree, piney ridge corner, fleur de lis border punches - Red and Black gel pens, Pink and Brown chalk, ½" letter stickers

Bat & Moon - ⅞" birch leaf, ⅞" cat, 1" oval, ⁵⁄₁₆" teardrop, romance lace border, 2" circle punches - Black and White gel pens, Gray chalk

Small Pumpkin - 1⅜" apple, ¾" hot air balloon, ⁵⁄₁₆" spiral, ½" maple leaf punches - Black and Brown gel pens, Black chalk

Ghost in Cauldron - 2" circle, 1⅞" cloud, 1⅛" smiley face, ¼" oval, ⅜" apple, ⅝" footprint, ¼" moon, ⅜" maple leaf, ½" maple leaf, ⅝" bat, ¼" spiral, ¼" star punches - Black gel pen, Orange and Black chalk

Large Pumpkin - 2" apple, ⁵⁄₁₆" circle, 1" circle, ½" pawprint, ½" spiral, ¾" maple leaf, ³⁄₁₆" square punches - Black and Brown gel pens, Black, Green, Orange and Brown chalk

Small Bat - 1¼" holly leaf, 1" cat, ½" oval, 1⅛" smiley face punches - Black and Green gel pens

We're 'batty' about Halloween!

Medium Bat - 1⅞" maple leaf, 1" cat, 1" oval, 1⅛" smiley face punches - Black and Green gel pens

Boo Ghost - 2" circle, oval cartoon bubble, 1⅝" bear, 1⅛" pumpkin, ½" maple leaf, ¼" oval, ⁵⁄₁₆" oval, ½" oval, ⅛" circle, ³⁄₁₆" circle, ¼" circle, ¾" circle, ⅞" rectangle, ⅞" birch leaf, grass border punches - Black and Gray gel pens, Orange, Gray, Blue and Black chalk

Owl - 2" circle, $\frac{7}{8}$" birch leaf, $\frac{3}{8}$" maple leaf, $1\frac{1}{4}$" scallop oval, 1" bear, $\frac{1}{4}$" diamond, $\frac{1}{2}$" snowflake punches - Hand cut branch, Black gel pen, Brown chalk

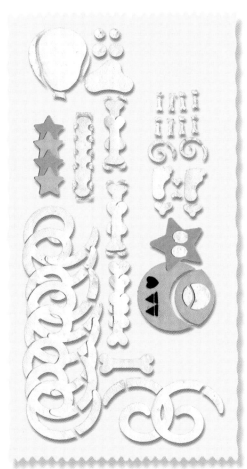

Make me dance with bone and paw punches!

Dancing Skeleton - 1" balloon, $\frac{3}{8}$" pawprint, $1\frac{1}{4}$" pawprint, $\frac{1}{8}$" circle, $\frac{3}{16}$" circle, $\frac{1}{4}$" circle, $\frac{1}{2}$" circle, $1\frac{1}{4}$" circle, $\frac{1}{2}$" star, 1" star, $\frac{1}{2}$" spiral, $1\frac{1}{4}$" spiral, 1" bone, $\frac{5}{8}$" footprint, $\frac{1}{4}$" bone, $\frac{3}{16}$" triangle, $\frac{3}{16}$" heart, $\frac{5}{16}$" oval, cloud cartoon bubble, $1\frac{1}{2}$" rectangle punches - Black gel pen, Gray chalk

Cowboys

Sheriff's Badge -
1" snowflake, 1/8" circle, 5/16" circle, 3/16" star punches

Six Shooter - 7/8" footprint, 7/16" cross, 1/8" circle, 3/16" circle, 3/16" star, 5/16" oval punches - Black gel pen, Brown chalk

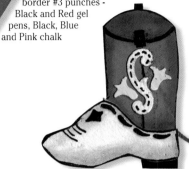

Stick Horse - 1½" mitten, 1⅛" footprint, 1/8" circle, 3/16" circle, 3/4" circle, 1/2" star, 3/16" birch leaf, 1½" rectangle, swirl border #1, swirl border #3 punches - Black and Red gel pens, Black, Blue and Pink chalk

Tepee - 1¾" pine tree, 1/4" cross, 1/2" triangle, 1/4" sun, 1/4" moon, city lights corner punches - Brown and Black chalk

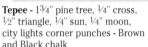

Horseshoe - 1/8" circle, 1" circle, 1½" circle, 3/8" square punches - Black gel pen, Black chalk

Log Cabin - 1¾" snowflake, 1⅞" flower, 7/8" rectangle, 1½" rectangle, 1/8" heart, 1/8" circle, 1" circle, swirl border #2, ivy border punches - Black and Brown gel pens, Black and Brown chalk

Cowboy Hat - 1⅞" oval, 1⅛" apple, 3/16" star punches - Black gel pen, Brown chalk

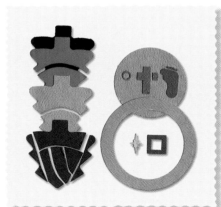

Gun Belt - 1¼" pine tree, 1/8" circle, 3/16" circle, 1½" circle, 2" circle, 1/4" square, 3/8" square, 5/8" star ornament, 7/16" cross, 5/8" footprint punches - Black and Brown gel pens, Brown chalk

Campfire - 2" circle, 1/2" oval, 1¼" maple leaf, 1⅞" maple leaf, 1/4" spiral, butterflies border punches - Black, Gray, Red and Orange gel pens, Brown, Black, Red and Orange chalk

Camping

Cowboy Boot - 2" heart, 1/4" rectangle, 3/8" square, 1/4" flower, 1/4" sun, baroque border, swirl border #3 punches - Black gel pen, Black chalk

Oval Bobber - 1/2" oval, fishing rod border punches - Black and Red gel pens, Black and Gray chalk

Round Bobber - 5/8" circle, 3/16" square punches - Black and Red gel pens, Black and Gray chalk

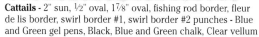

Fishing Lure - 1 1/16" fleur de lis, 3/8" pawprint, crown border, Vivaldi border punches - Black gel pen, Black chalk

Cattails - 2" sun, 1/2" oval, 1 7/8" oval, fishing rod border, fleur de lis border, swirl border #1, swirl border #2 punches - Blue and Green gel pens, Black, Blue and Green chalk, Clear vellum

Fishermoose - Rectangle cartoon bubble, 1" balloon, 1 3/16" heart, 3/4" hawthorn leaf, 1/8" circle, 1/2" circle, 3/4" circle, 1 1/4" circle, fishing rod border, 1 1/8" fish, 1/2" oval, 1" oval, 7/8" rectangle, Vivaldi border, 3/8" birch leaf punches - Black, Brown, Green and Fuchsia gel pens, Black, Brown, Yellow and Green chalk

Cherries - 1¼" holly, ½" circle, ⅝" birch leaf, grandma's lace border punches - Black and Brown gel pens, Black and Brown chalk

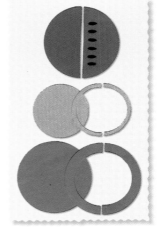

Watermelon Slice - 1¼" circle, 1½" circle, 2" circle, heart and tears border punches - Black and White gel pens, Green, Black and Purple chalk

Strawberry - 1⅛" apple, ¾" palm tree punches - Black and White gel pens, Green and Purple chalk

Flower Vase - ⅝" heart, ⁵⁄₁₆" oval, ½" oval, 1⅞" oval, ⅝" birch leaf, ½" circle punches - Hand cut stems, Black gel pen, Green chalk, Swirl pattern vellum

Topiary - ¾" dusty miller leaf, 1½" rectangle, 1½" circle, ⅞" bow punches - Black gel pen, Black, Yellow, Brown and Orange chalk

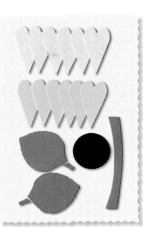

Sunflower - ½" primitive heart, ⅞" impatiens leaf, ¾" circle punches - Hand cut stem, Green gel pen, Green, Brown and Yellow chalk

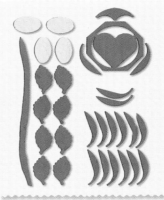

Corn - ½" oval, ⅝" birch leaf, 1" frame heart punches - Hand cut stem, Black and Light Brown gel pens, Brown chalk

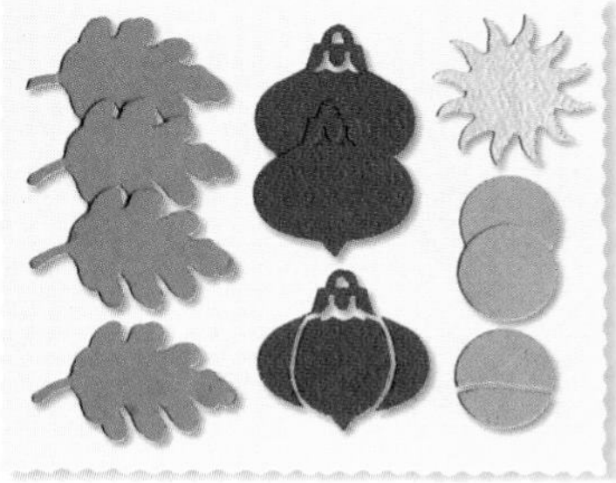

Acorns - ¾" hawthorn leaf, 1" oval ornament, 1" sun, ⅝" circle punches - Black, Brown and Green gel pens, Black, Brown, Rust and Green chalk

Tree with Branches - 1¼" holly, ⅝" cloud punches - Brown chalk

Pine cone Swag - 1" tree, ⅝" teardrop, ¼" oval, ⁵⁄₁₆" oval, ½" circle, ¼" moon, swirl border #1, swirl border #2 punches - Black and Brown gel pens, Brown and Green chalk

Medium Tree - 1" balloon, 1¼" scallop oval punches - Green and Black chalk

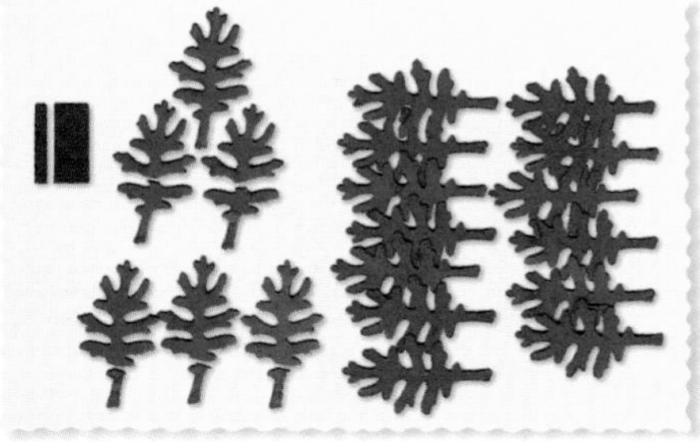

Fir Tree - ¾" dusty miller leaf, ½" rectangle punches - Black gel pen

Large Tree - 1⅞" oval, 1⅞" cloud punches - Green, and Black chalk

Tree with Swing - 1⅞" flower, ⁵⁄₁₆" circle, ⅝"circle, ¾" square, 1⅞" maple leaf punches - Brown gel pen, Green and Brown chalk

Apple Tree - 1⅞" flower, 1⅞" oval, ³⁄₁₆" circle punches - Green and Black chalk

Nature

Bluebird - 1¼" scallop oval, ½" circle, ⅞" birch leaf, ¼" diamond, ½" snowflake, baroque border punches - Black and White gel pens, Blue chalk

Smiling Flower - Rectangle cartoon bubble, 1½" rectangle, 1⁹/₁₆" square, swirl border #1, 1" oval, 1" circle, 1¼" circle, ⅞" impatiens leaf, ½" primitive heart, ³/₁₆" heart, 1⅛" smiley face, ⅜" square punches - Black gel pen, Yellow, Purple, Green and Black chalk

Pine Tree & Moon - 1⁷/₁₆" heart, 2" heart, ¾" circle, 1¼" circle, ⅜" star punches - Black gel pen, Black and Yellow chalk

Bugs in a Jar - 2" circle, 1⅛" dragonfly punches - Hand cut 3⅜" circle, Black, Green and Brown gel pens, Green and Black chalk, Clear vellum

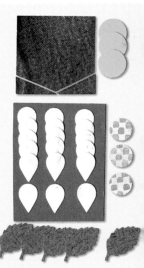

Pocket Full of Posies - 1⁹/₁₆" square, ½" circle, ⅝" circle, ⅝" birch leaf, ⅝" teardrop punches - Black gel pen, Orange, Gray, Green and Black chalk
Hint: Glue teardrop on ⅝" circles. Top with ½" circles to make these delightful daisies.

Smiling Sun - 1⅞" cloud, 2" sun, ⅛" circle, 1" circle, 1⅛" smiley face punches - Orange, Black and White gel pens, Blue and Rust chalk

Rose - 1⅞" oval, rectangle cartoon bubble, ⅞" impatiens leaf, ⅝" sun, ½" swirl, swirl border #1 punches - Black gel pen, Green and Black chalk

Beehive - 1" flower, 1¼" flower, 1½" flower, 1⅞" flower, ½" circle punches - Black gel pen, Light Brown chalk

Apple with Worm - 2" apple, ⅝" birch leaf, 5/16" diamond, 1¼" spiral punches - Black, Green, Red and Brown gel pens, Green and Black chalk
Hint: Trim the left over space after punching a spiral to make a worm.

Bumblebee - ½" oval, ¼" bone, 1" oval punches - Black gel pen, Light Brown and Pink chalk, Clear vellum

Garden Marker - 3/16" circle, 1" frame heart, 1½" rectangle, ¾" square, city lights corner, 1" oval, grass border punches - Hand cut 1⅝" x 1⅛" rectangle and 3¼" x ⅛" strip, Black and Brown gel pens, Gray and Brown chalk

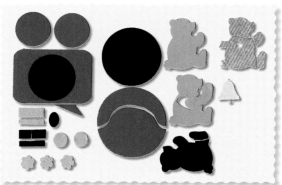

Bear on Tractor - Rectangle cartoon bubble, 1" side bear, ⅝" bell, ½" rectangle, 5/16" circle, ¾" circle, 1" circle, 1¼" circle, 1½" circle, 5/16" oval, ¼" flower punches - Brown gel pen, Gray, Black, Brown, Blue and Pink chalk

Farm Day

Haystack - 2" circle, ¼" cross punches - Brown gel pen, Brown chalk

Nesting Hen - 1¼" maple leaf, ¾" palm tree, ⅝" teardrop, ⅜" heart, ⅜" flower, 3/16" triangle, 7/16" cross punches - Black, Brown and Gray gel pens, Brown, Gray and Black chalk

Sheep - 1" flower, 1¼" scallop oval, ⅝" egg, 1⅛" bow punches - Pink and Blue gel pens, Gray chalk

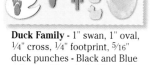

Duck Family - 1" swan, 1" oval, ¼" cross, ¼" footprint, 5/16" duck punches - Black and Blue gel pens, Blue chalk, Blue vellum

Rooster - 1" oval, ⅞" footprint, ⅝" teardrop, ⅜" birch leaf, 5/16" flower, 5/16" diamond, ½" snowflake, ½" sun, swirl border #2 punches - Black gel pen, Brown and Black chalk

Turkey Gobbler - 1¼" balloon, ⅝" teardrop, ⅝" birch leaf, ¼" diamond, ¼" oval, swirl border #2, ½" snowflake, ⅝" cloud, 1" flower punches - Black gel pen, Brown and Black chalk

Farm
Day

Farmer's Wife - 1¼" scallop oval, ½" bow, 1/16" circle, ⅞" footprint, 1" bell, 1" flower, ½" heart, ⅝" heart, ¼" flower punches - Red, Black, Gold gel pens, Blue, Gray, Pink chalk

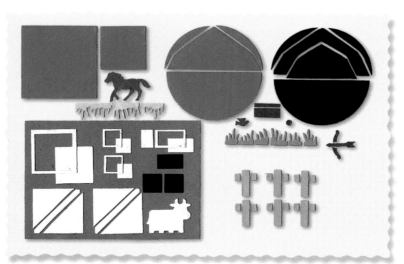

Barn & Corral - 5/16" square, ⅜" square, ¾" square, ⅞" square, 1 9/16" square, ½" rectangle, ⅞" rectangle, grass border, 7/16" cross, ⅞" cow, 1" horse, ⅛" circle, 2" circle, ⅝" bow and arrow, ¼" bird punches - Black and Brown gel pens, Brown, Pink and Black chalk

Farmer - ⅞" footprint, ⅞" bell, 1" bell, 1" flower, ½" heart, ⅝" heart, 1" frame tulip, ½" maple leaf, ⅞" rectangle punches - Brown, Black and Gold gel pens, Gray, Blue and Brown chalk

Cow Border - Checker border, ½" primitive heart, 1" oval, ⅞" cow, 1" snowflake, ½" tulip, ¼" tulip punches - Brown, Black and Gold gel pens, Gray, Blue and Brown chalk

'Foot' Animals

Basic Footprint Animal Body - ⅞" footprint, 1⅛" footprint, 1¼" footprint, 1¾" footprint, ⅝" egg, 3/16" birch leaf, swirl borders #1 & 2, ⅛" circle punches

Saddle & Bridle - (Basic body), ¾" square, ⅝" teardrop, swirl border #2, ⅝" footprint, 3/16" circle punches **-** Black gel pen, Brown and Black chalk

Lion - (Basic body), 1½" sun, 3/16" circle, ¼" circle, 5/16" circle, ¼" pawprint, ¼" footprint, 1¼" spiral punches **-** Black gel pen, Brown chalk

Bear - (Basic body), 1" balloon head, ½" circle, 5/16" circle, ½" oval, ⅝" strawberry, ⅝" footprint, ½" pawprint, 1⅛" smiley face punches **-** Black and Red gel pens, Brown and Black chalk

Ladybug - 1¾" footprint for head, ⅝" footprint for feet, 3/16" circle, ¼" circle, 1½" circle, 1⅛" smiley face for mouth, swirl border #4 punches **-** Black gel pen, Black chalk

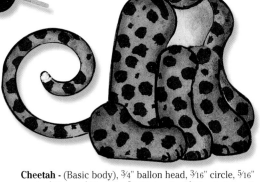

Tiger - (Basic body), 3/16" circle, 5/16" circle, fleur de lis border, 3/16" triangle, 1¼" spiral punches **-** Black gel pen, Black and Gray chalk

Cheetah - (Basic body), ¾" ballon head, 3/16" circle, 5/16" circle, ¼" sun, ½" apple, 3/16" triangle, 1¼" spiral punches **-** Black and White gel pens, Black, Pink and Gray chalk

Monkey - (Basic body), ⅝" footprint & ⅞" footprint for arms, feet & legs, 3/16" circle, 5/16" circle, ½" circle, ⅝" circle, ¼" oval, ½" oval, ⅝" banana, ½" rectangle, 15/16" spiral, ¼" hand, 1⅛" smiley face punches **-** Black, Red & Green gel pens, Black, Brown & Pink chalk

Zebra - (Basic body), grass border, ¼" footprint, 3/16" circle punches - Black gel pen, Black chalk

Mule - (Basic body), grass border, ⅜" birch leaf, 1" oval, ½" primitive heart, ¼" rectangle, 1⅛" smiley face punches - Black and White gel pens, Black, Brown, Gray and Pink chalk

Giraffe - (Basic body), grass border, ¼" footprint, ¼" rectangle, 3/16" circle punches - Black gel pen, Brown and Orange chalk

Reindeer - (Basic body), ¼" oval, 5/16" oval, ½" oval, 1" oval, ½" pawprint, ¾" dusty miller leaf, ⅜" birch leaf punches - Black, Brown and White gel pens, Black and Brown chalk
Hint: Change the direction of animal legs to make us move.

Gator - (Basic body), untrimmed ⅞" footprint for legs and 1¼" footprint for head, 3/16" circle, 5/16" circle, 5/16" diamond, 3/16" heart punches - Black gel pen, Pink and Green chalk
Hint: Trim leftover space after punching a 2¼" spiral for tail.

Camel - (Basic body), 1 7/16" heart, ¼" sun, ⅝" sun, ⅛" heart, ¼" footprint, 1⅛" smiley face punches - Black and Brown gel pens, Brown, Black and Pink chalk

'Foot' Animals

Elephant - (Basic body), $1^7/16$" heart and 2" heart for head and ears, $1/4$" heart for trunk, $1/8$" heart, $3/16$" heart, $1/4$" footprint punches - Black and Pink gel pens, Black chalk

Hippo - (Basic body), $1^1/4$" balloon for head, $5/8$" strawberry, $5/8$" circle, $3/16$" square, $1/4$" oval, $1^1/8$" smiley face punches - Pink, Black and Red gel pens, Pink and Black chalk

'Foot' Animals make great accents for Scrapbook Pages... 'Day at the Zoo' or 'Day at the Farm'!

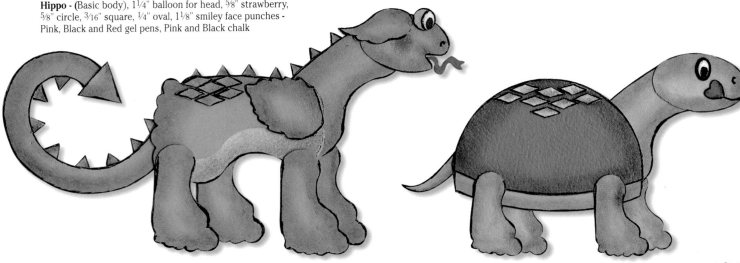

Dragon - (Basic body), $1^1/8$" footprint for legs, 1" swan for ear, 1" oval for head, $1/4$" circle, $3/16$" triangle, $1/2$" triangle, $7/8$" birch leaf, $5/16$" diamond, celebration border, $2^1/4$" swirl punches - Black and White gel pens, Pink, Green and Brown chalk

Turtle - (Basic body), 2" circle for shell, $7/8$" footprint for legs, 1" oval for head, $3/16$" heart, $5/16$" diamond, $1^1/8$" smiley face punches - Black gel pen, Green and Black chalk

tterfly - (Basic body), ³⁄₁₆" circle, ½" circle, rl border #4 punches - Black gel pen, Yellow, k, Purple and Black chalk

Wolf - (Basic body), ⁵⁄₈"strawberry, ⅛" heart, ¼" heart, ¼" country heart, ³⁄₈" birch leaf, ⅞" birch leaf, 1⅛" smiley face punches - Black and White gel pens, Black, Pink and Gray chalk

Pig - (Basic body), 1" balloon for head, ⁵⁄₈" strawberry, ½" spiral, ³⁄₁₆" circle, ⁵⁄₈" circle, 1³⁄₁₆" heart, ⁵⁄₈" teardrop, 1⅛" smiley face punches - Black gel pen, Black and Pink chalk

Cow - (Basic body), ¾" balloon and 1" oval for head, ⁵⁄₁₆" teardrop for ears, ¼" oval, ½" oval, ¼" moon, ⁷⁄₁₆" bell, ¼" spiral, ¼" footprint, ¼" hand, ⁵⁄₈" circle, ¼" sun, ¼" lips, grass border punches - White, Purple, Brown and Black gel pens, Gray and Brown chalk

p - (Basic body), 1" oval for head, ½" or ears, layer two 1¾" footprints for ¼" spiral, ⁵⁄₁₆" spiral punches - gel pen, Pink and Black chalk

Poodle - (Basic body), ⁵⁄₈" cloud, ⁵⁄₈" teardrop, ⅛" heart, ¼" spiral, ⁵⁄₁₆" spiral, ¹⁵⁄₁₆" spiral, 1⅛" smiley face punches - Black gel pen, Black chalk

Mouse - (Basic body), 1³⁄₁₆" heart, ½" circle, ⁵⁄₈" circle, ¼" oval, fleur de lis border, ³⁄₈" pawprint, ½" pawprint, 1¼" spiral, ½" rectangle, ⅞" rectangle, 1¼" scallop oval, 1⅛" smiley face punches - Black and Brown gel pens, Pink, Black and Gray chalk

It's fun to make a fish that looks like it is swimming in a Vellum fishbowl!

Fishbowl & Gold Fish - ¼" circle, ⅜" circle, 1½" circle, 2" circle, grass border, swirl border #2, ⅝" shell, 1" oval, 1" grape leaf, ⅜" birch leaf, ¼" lips punches **-** Black and Blue gel pens, Black, Orange and Blue chalk, Clear vellum

Palm Tree - ⁵⁄₁₆" circle, 2" circle, ⅞" birch leaf punches **-** Brown gel pen, Brown and Green chalk

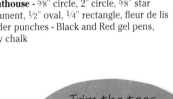
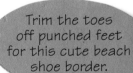

Lighthouse - ⅝" circle, 2" circle, ⅝" star ornament, ½" oval, ¼" rectangle, fleur de lis border punches **-** Black and Red gel pens, Gray chalk

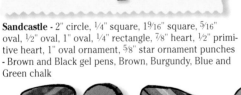

Trim the toes off punched feet for this cute beach shoe border.

Sandcastle - 2" circle, ¼" square, 1⁹⁄₁₆" square, ⁵⁄₁₆" oval, ½" oval, 1" oval, ¼" rectangle, ⅞" heart, ½" primitive heart, 1" oval ornament, ⅝" star ornament punches **-** Brown and Black gel pens, Brown, Burgundy, Blue and Green chalk

Flip-Flop Sandals Border - 1⅛" footprint punch **-** Black gel pen

Sand Pail - 1⁹/₁₆" square, rectangle cartoon bubble, cloud cartoon bubble, ³/₁₆" circle, 1¼" circle, 1½" circle, ³/₈" star punches - Brown and Black gel pens, Black and Brown chalk

Frog - 1¾" butterfly, ³/₁₆" circle, ¼" circle, ½" circle, ⁵/₈" circle, 1½" circle, 2" circle, 2" heart, 1⅛" smiley face, 1" frame tulip, 1" oval punches - Black gel pen, Pink, Green and Yellow chalk, White gel pen

Beach Sandals - 1¾" footprint punch - Black gel pen, Yellow, Blue and Green chalk

Playing at the Beach is fun for all ages... palm trees, sandcastles, a lighthouse and memorabilia of ships.

Anchor - ¼" circle, ⁵/₁₆" circle, 2" circle, 1½" rectangle, 1⅛" fish punches - Black gel pen, Rust chalk

Porthole - ⅛" circle, 1½" circle, 2" circle punches - Black and White gel pens, Blue and Gray chalk, Blue vellum

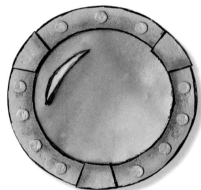

Shovel - ¼" square, ³/₈" square, ⁵/₈" square, ⁷/₈" rectangle punches - Gray and Black gel pens, Black chalk

Ship's Wheel - 1¾" snowflake, ³/₁₆" star, ⁵/₁₆" oval, ⁵/₁₆" circle, ½" circle, 1" circle, 1¼" circle punches - Black gel pen, Black chalk

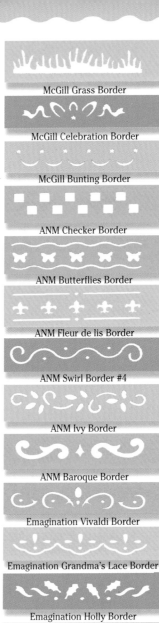

McGill Grass Border

McGill Celebration Border

McGill Bunting Border

ANM Checker Border

ANM Butterflies Border

ANM Fleur de lis Border

ANM Swirl Border #4

ANM Ivy Border

ANM Baroque Border

Emagination Vivaldi Border

Emagination Grandma's Lace Border

Emagination Holly Border

Emagination Romance Lace Border

FT Swirl Border #2

FT Swirl Border #3

FT Swirl Border #1

FT Heart & Tears Border

McGill Crown Border

McGill Fishing Rod Border

Nankong Cloud ⅝", 1⅞"

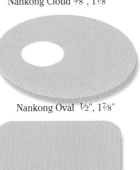

Nankong Oval ½", 1⅞"

Emagination Rectangle Cartoon Bubble

Emagination Oval Cartoon Bubble

Emagination Cloud Cartoon Bubble

Emagination Bow Corner

Emagination City Lights Corner

Emagination Piney Ridge Corner

Nankong 1" Bear

FT 1" Side Bear

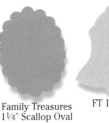

McGill 1⅛" Fish

McGill 1⅛" Dragonfly

Nankong 1⅛" Foot

McGill 1³⁄₁₆" Heart

Family Treasures 1¼" Scallop Oval

FT 1" Bell

McGill 1" Cat

Emagination 1" Oval

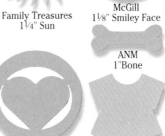

Family Treasures 1¼" Sun

McGill 1⅛" Smiley Face

McGill 1⅛" Pumpkin

Marvy 1" Flower

ANM 1" Frame Smiley

ANM 1" Bone

McGill 1" Frame Heart

Emagination 1" Dress

Hyglo ¾" Hot Air Balloon

McGill Balloon ⅝", 1"

Marvy Corner Rounder

McGill ⅞" Bell

Marvy Heart ½", ⅞", 1⁷⁄₁₆", 2"

Marvy Footprint ⅝", ⅞", 1¼", 1¾"

Marvy Flower ⁵⁄₁₆", ⅝", 1", 1½", 1⁷⁄₈"

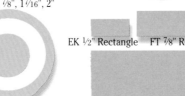

ANM Circle ⅝", 1", 1¼"

EK ½" Rectangle

FT ⅞" Rectangle

McGill 1¼" Pawprint

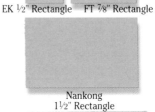

Nankong 1½" Rectangle

Marvy Circle ½", ¾", 1½", 2"

Family Treasures Square ⅛", ¼", ⁵⁄₁₆", ⅜", ½", ⁹⁄₁₆", ⅝", ¾", ¹⁵⁄₁₆", 1¼", 1⁹⁄₁₆"

Marvy Balloon ¾", 1¼", 1½", 2"